OWEN DAVEY
THE WHO'S WHO
OF GROWN-UPS

JOBS, HOBBIES, AND THE TOOLS IT TAKES

LITTLE
GESTALTEN

chef pants

ladle

toque blanche

saucepan

wooden spoon

neckerchief

tea towel

CHEF

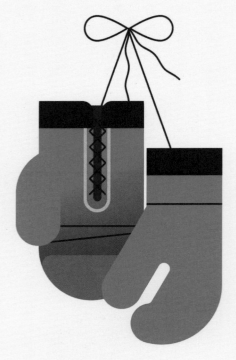

boxing gloves

championship belt

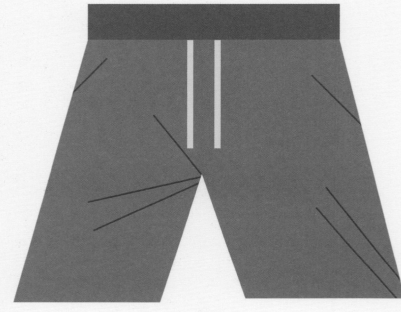

shorts

mouth guard

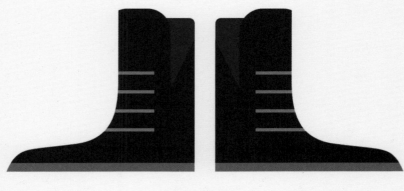

boots

BOXING CHAMPION

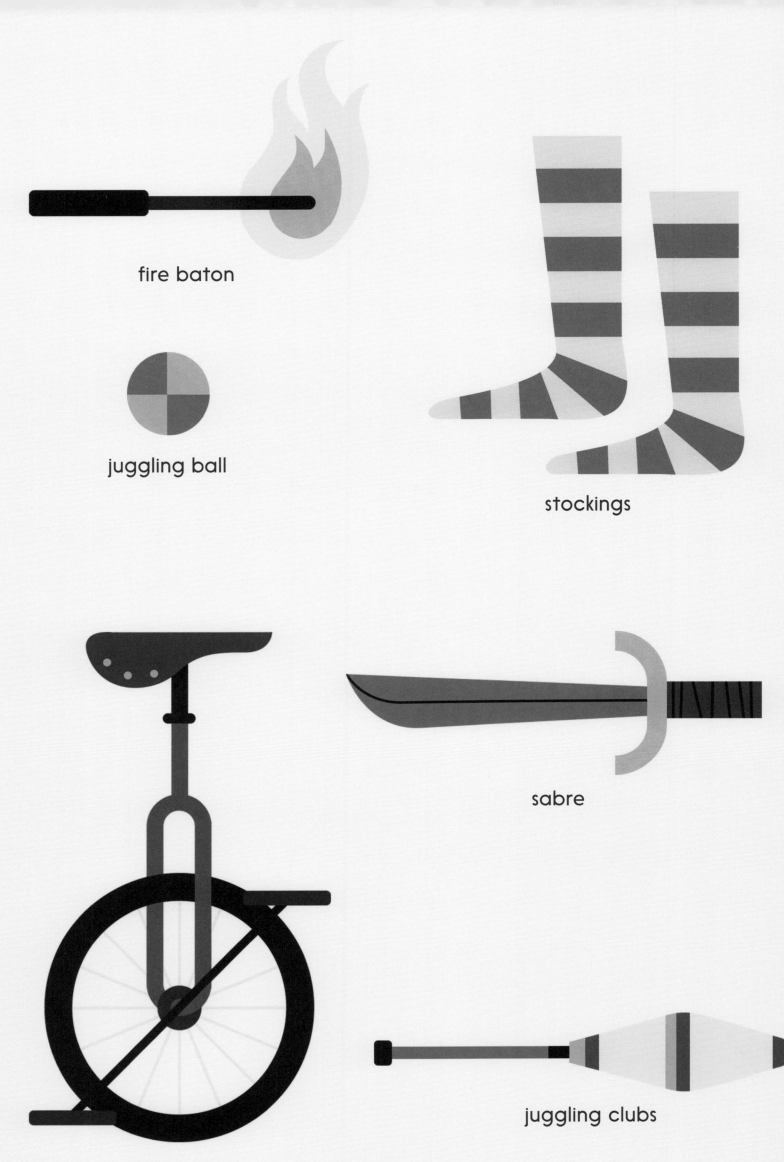

fire baton

juggling ball

stockings

unicycle

sabre

juggling clubs

JUGGLER

sailor cap

bundle

sailor shirt

sailor collar

badge

sailor overshirt

SAILOR

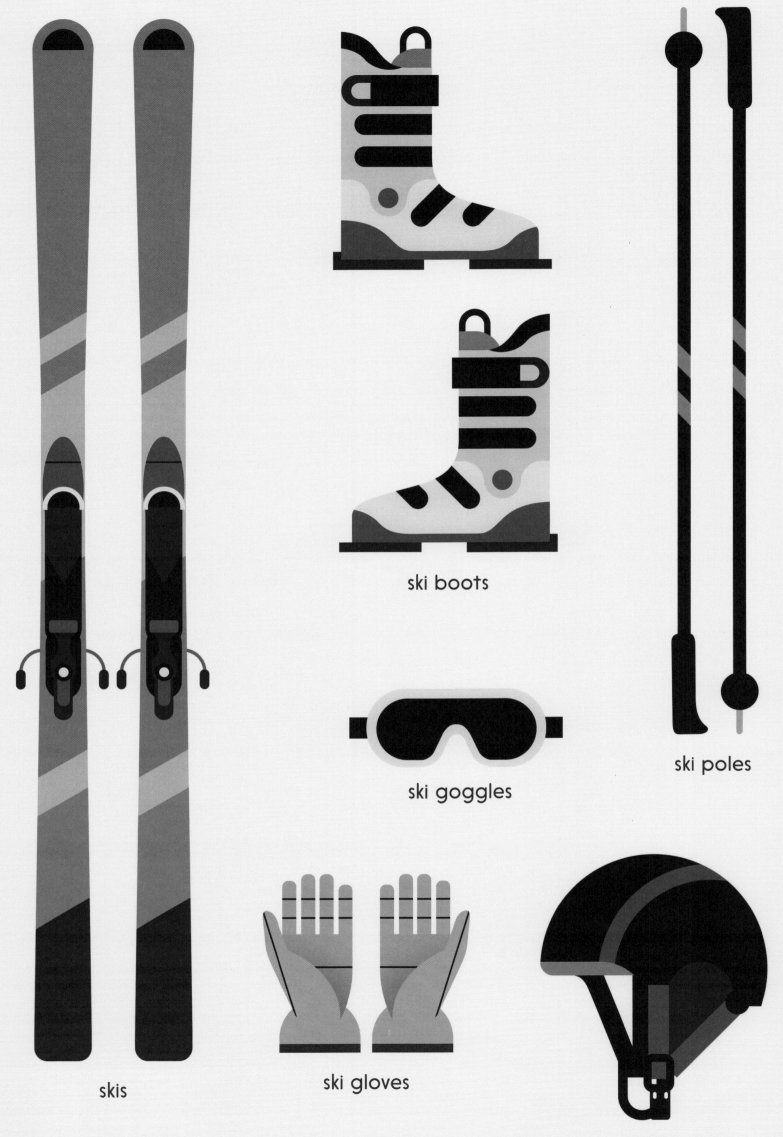

ski boots

ski goggles

ski poles

skis

ski gloves

helmet

SKIER

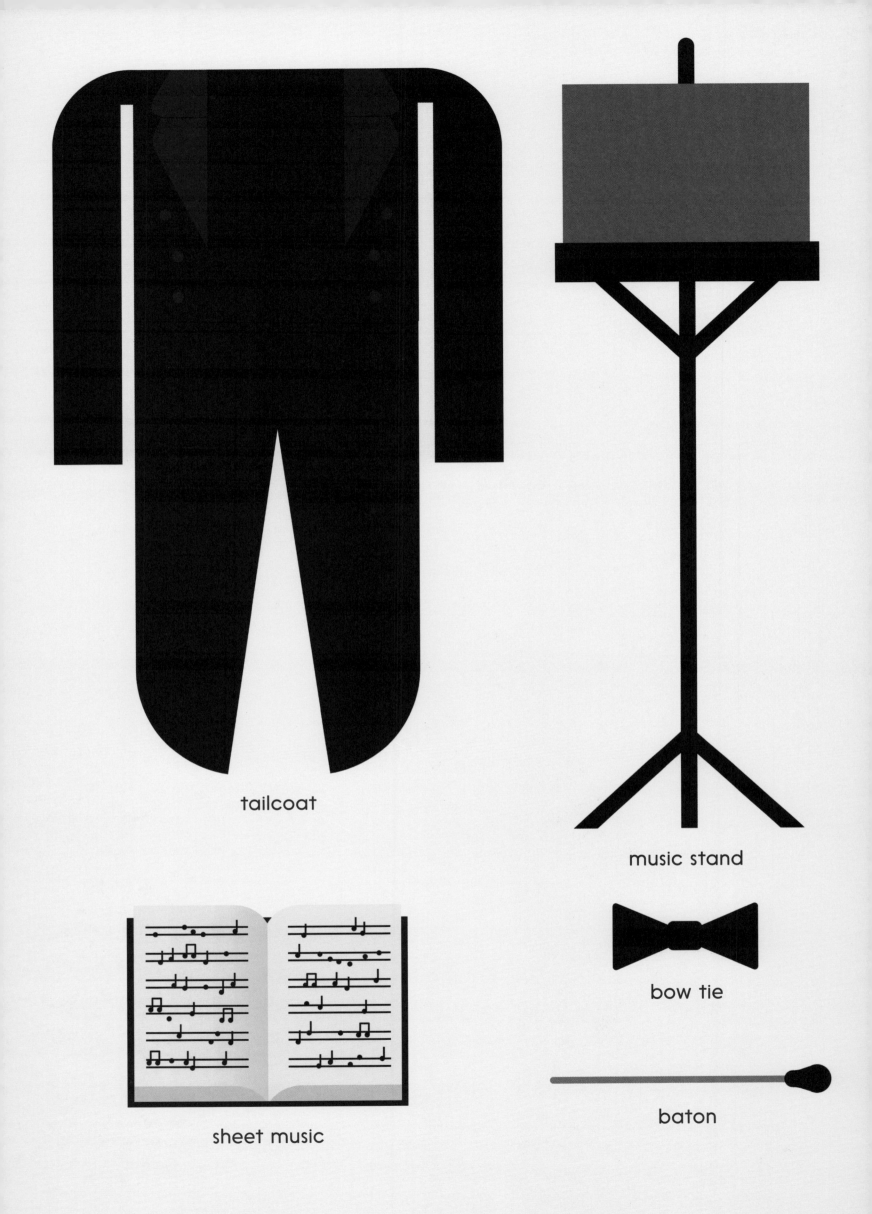

tailcoat

music stand

sheet music

bow tie

baton

CONDUCTOR

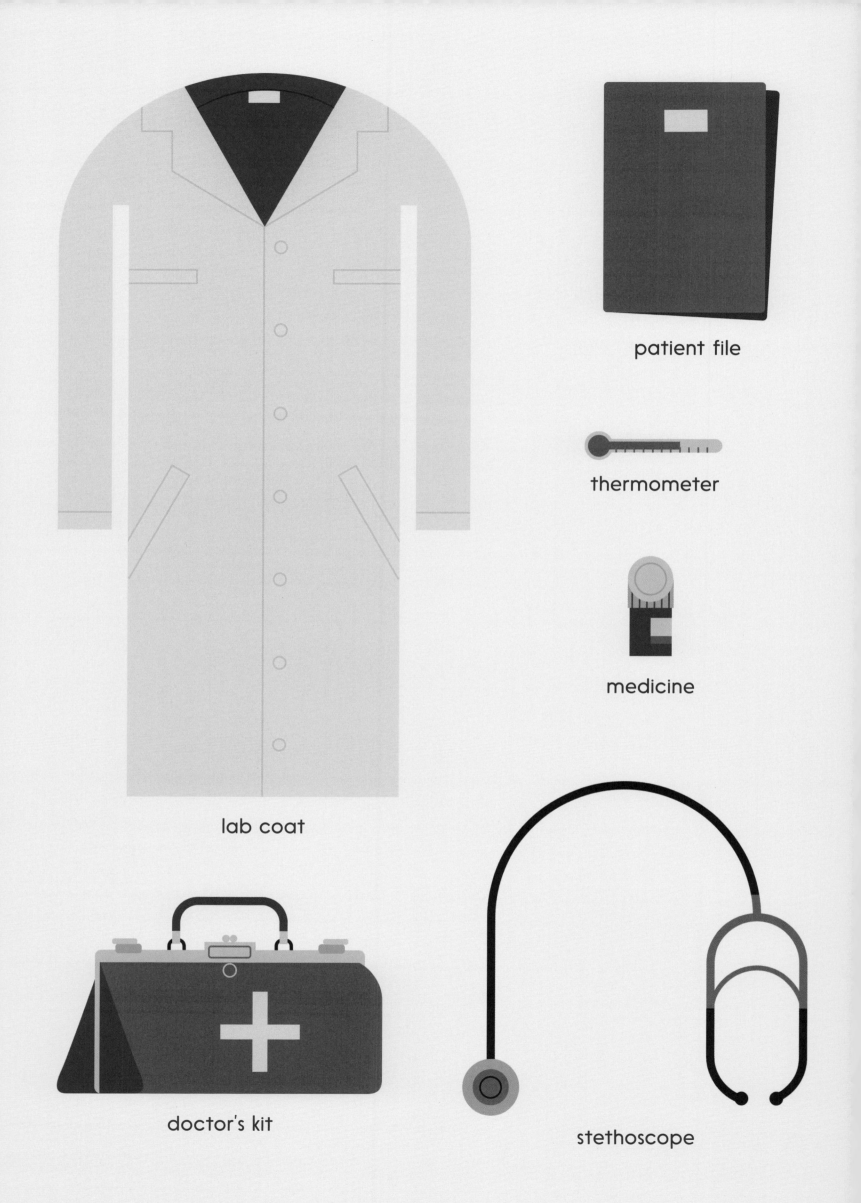

patient file

thermometer

medicine

lab coat

doctor's kit

stethoscope

DOCTOR

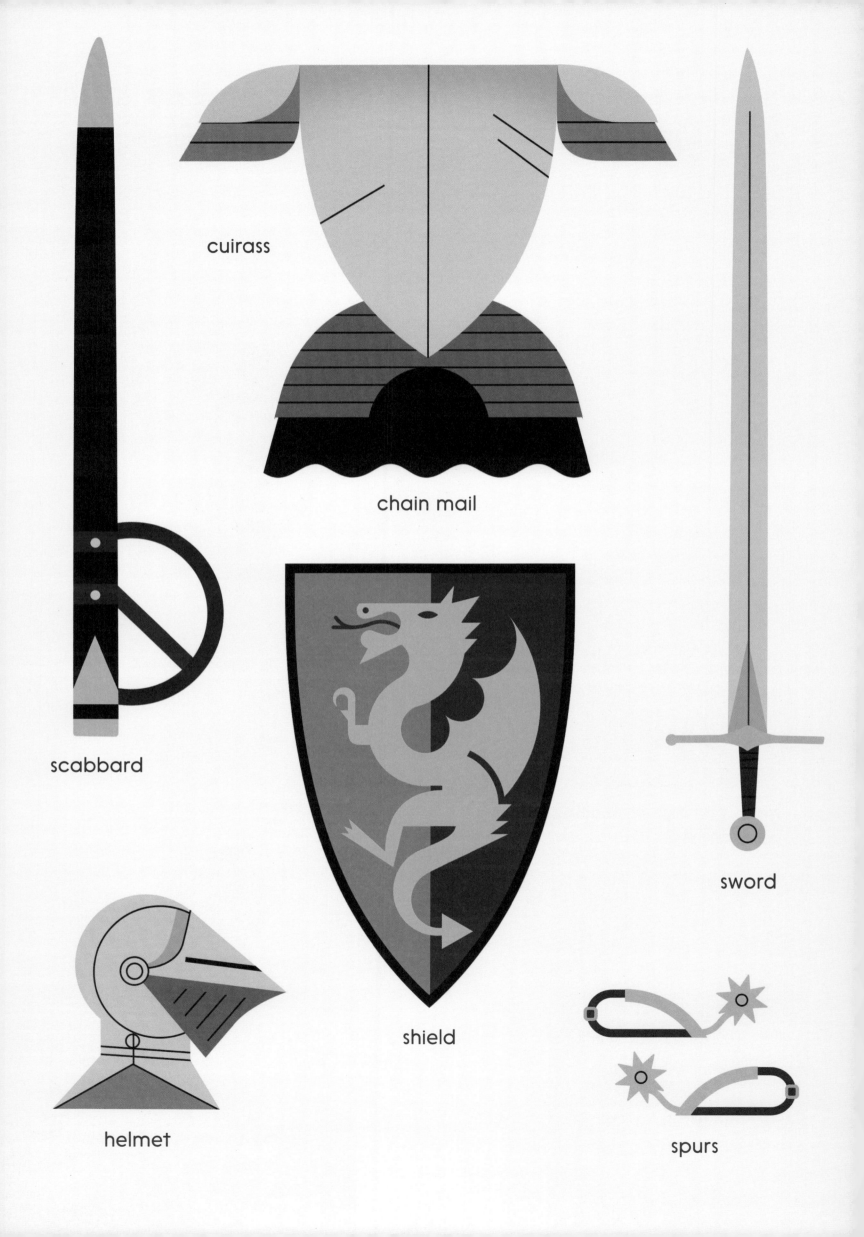

cuirass

chain mail

scabbard

shield

helmet

spurs

sword

KNIGHT

soccer shirt

soccer ball

shin guards

cleats

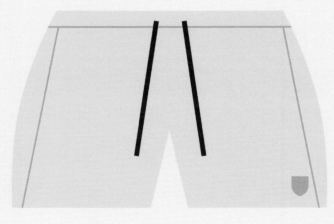

shorts

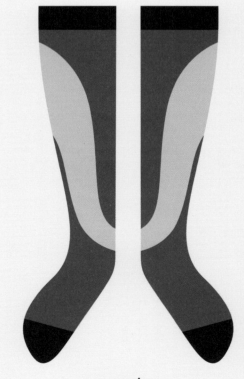

socks

SOCCER PLAYER

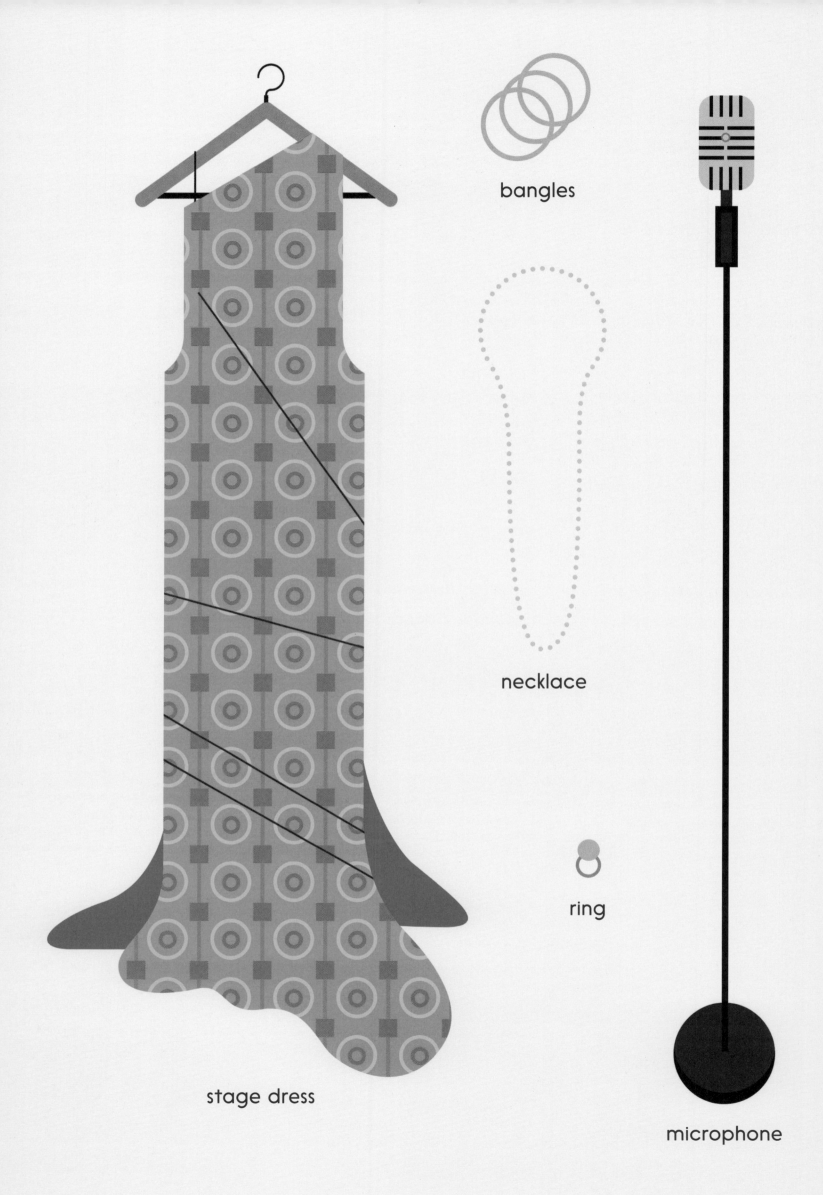

bangles

necklace

ring

microphone

stage dress

SINGER

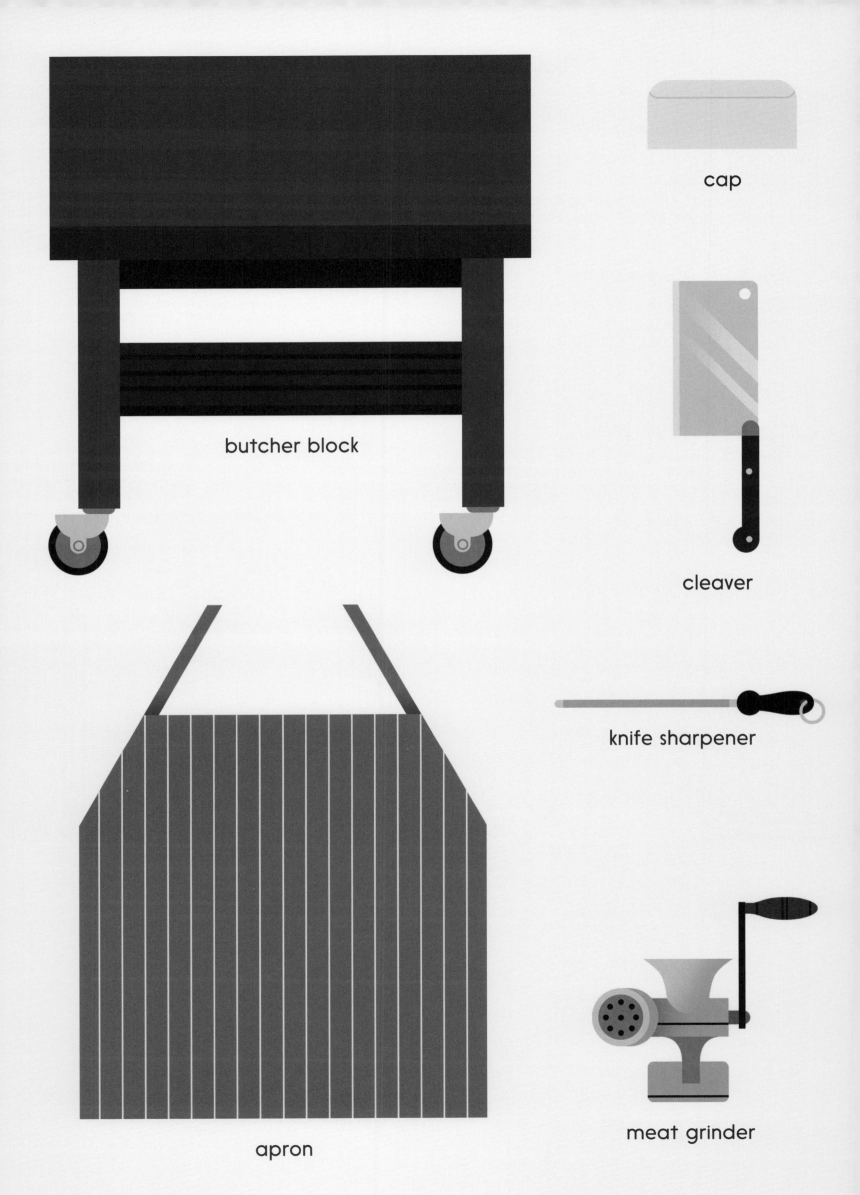

butcher block

apron

cap

cleaver

knife sharpener

meat grinder

BUTCHER

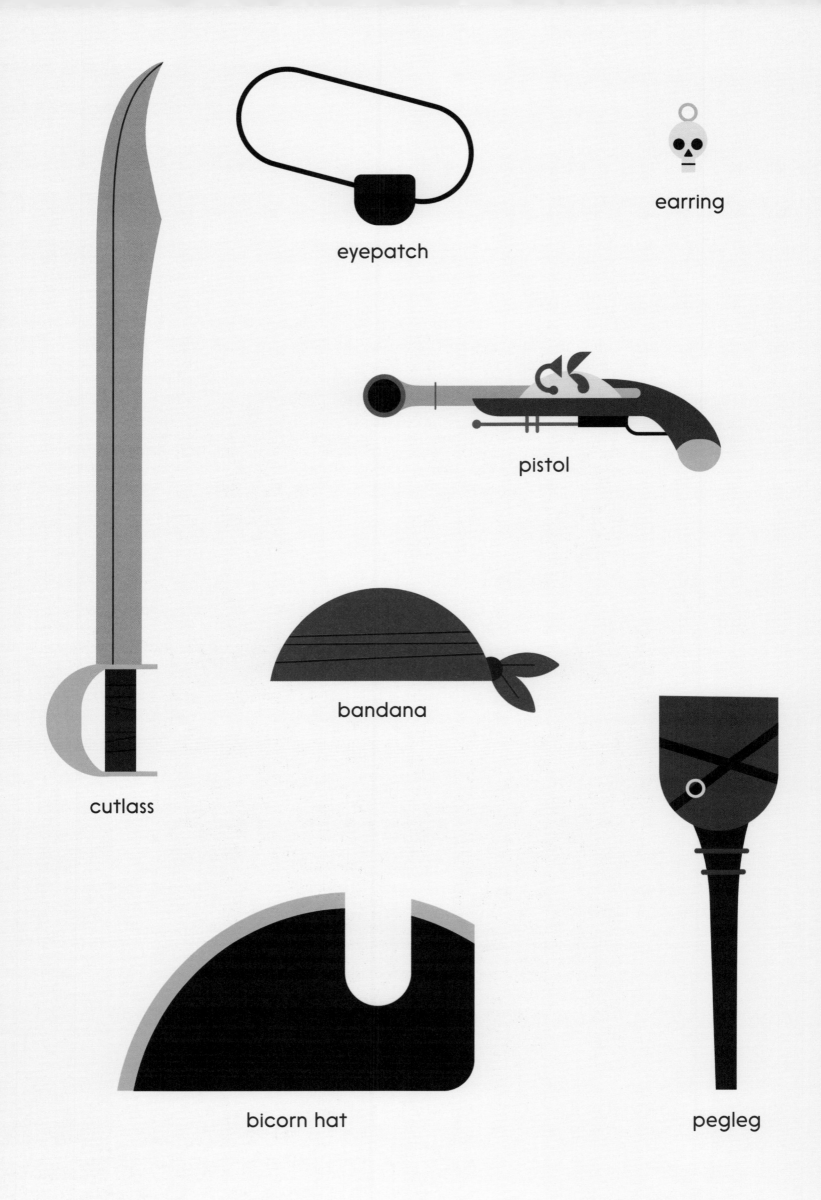

eyepatch

earring

pistol

cutlass

bandana

bicorn hat

pegleg

PIRATE

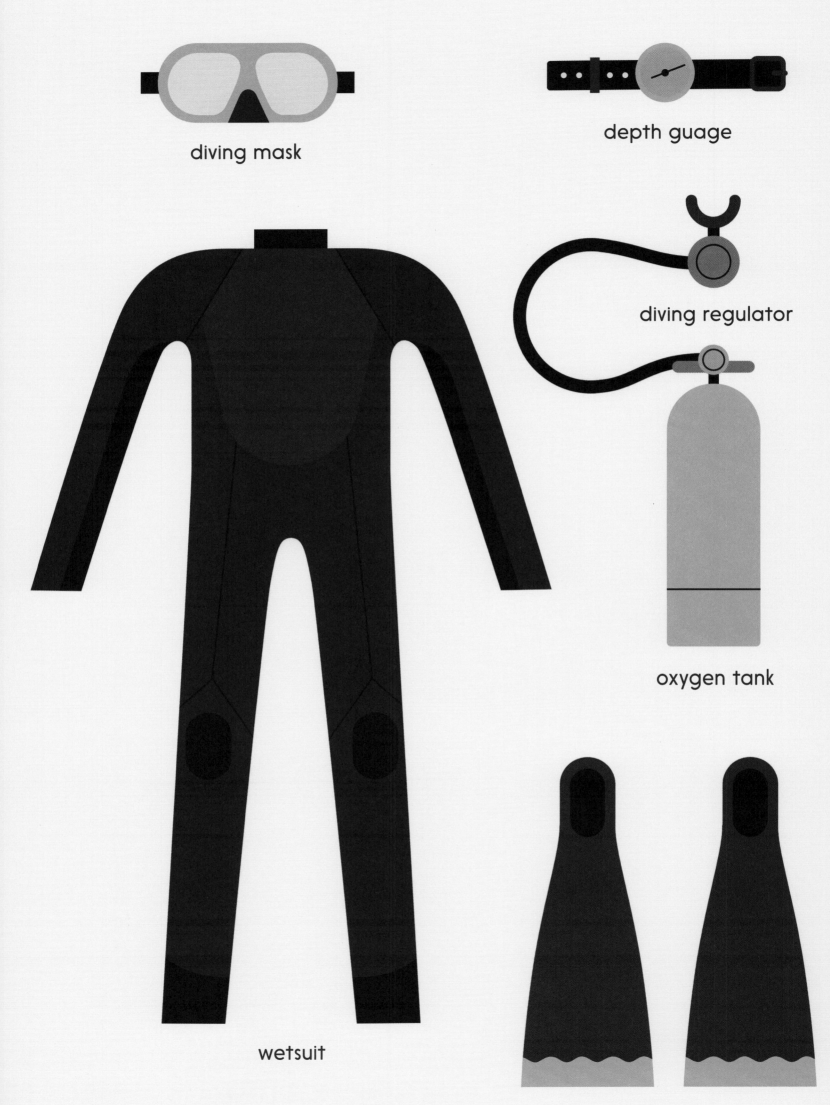

diving mask

depth guage

diving regulator

oxygen tank

wetsuit

flippers

DIVER

pistol with silencer

fedora

watch

trench coat

sunglasses

SECRET AGENT

knee pads

sneakers

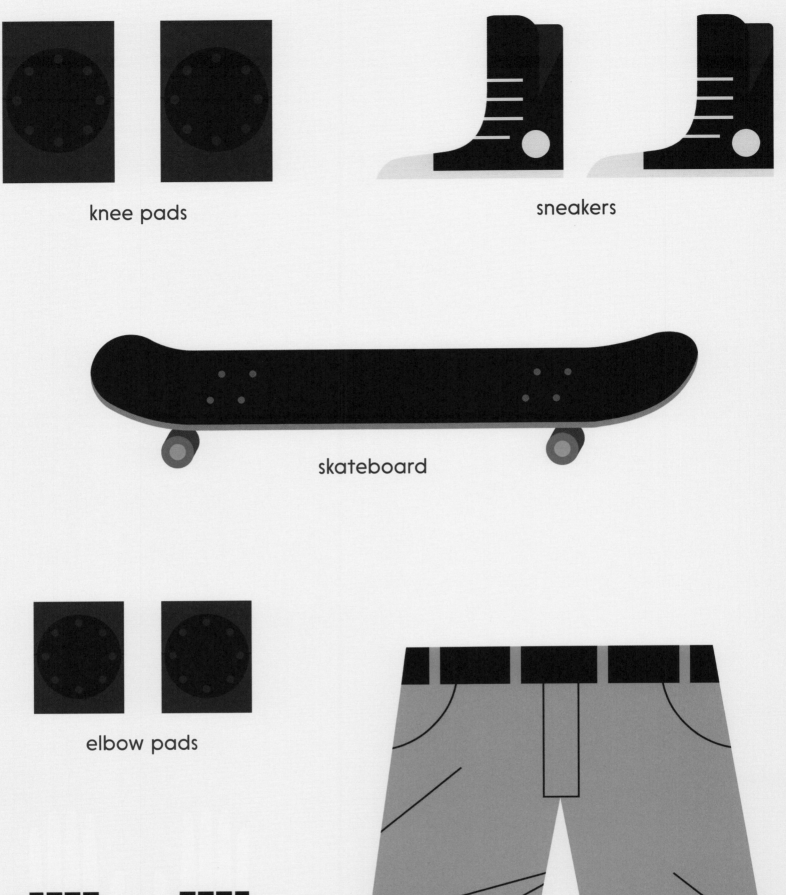

skateboard

elbow pads

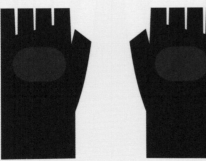

protective gloves

baggy pants

SKATER

belt pack

glasses

comic books

video game

headset

laptop

tote bag

NERD

dungarees

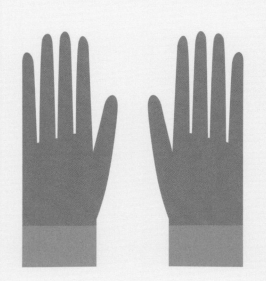

gardening gloves

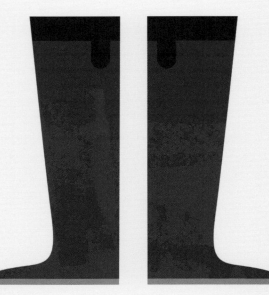

rubber boots

shovel

garden shears

cap

GARDENER

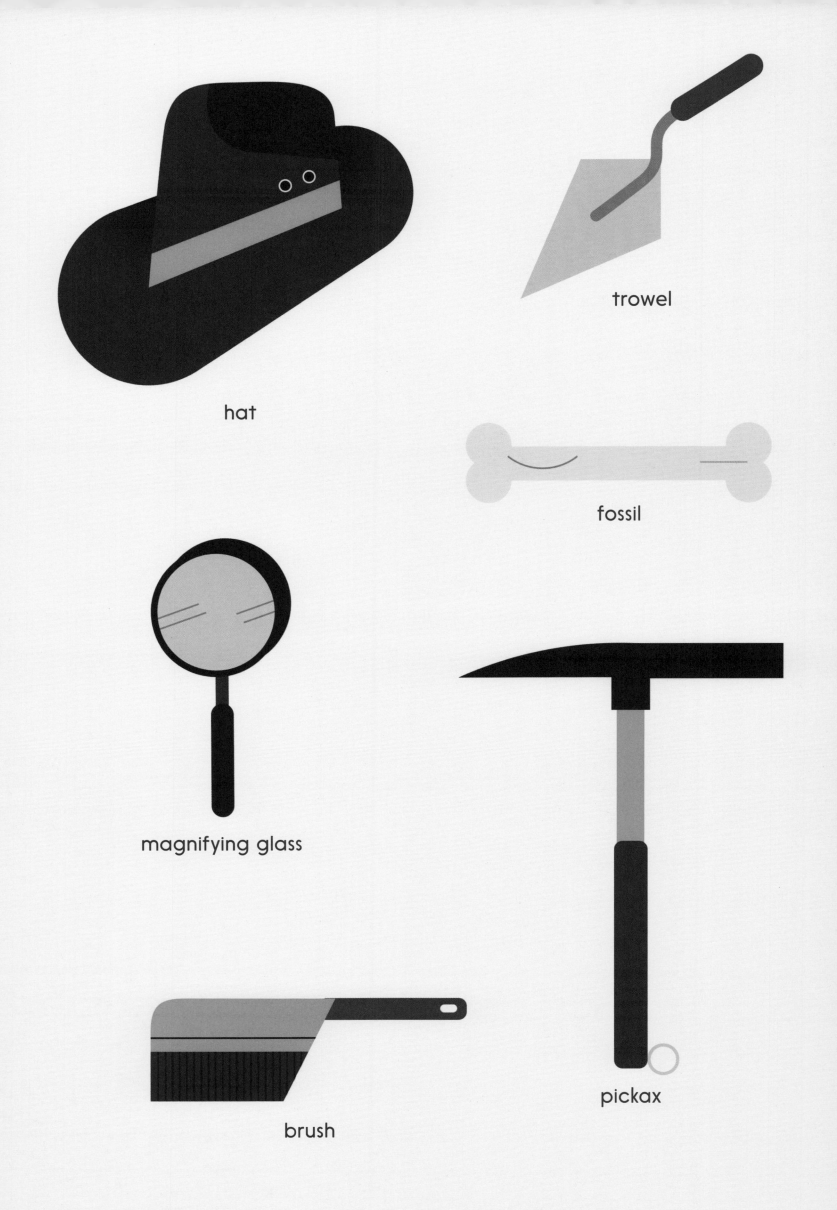

hat

trowel

fossil

magnifying glass

pickax

brush

ARCHAEOLOGIST

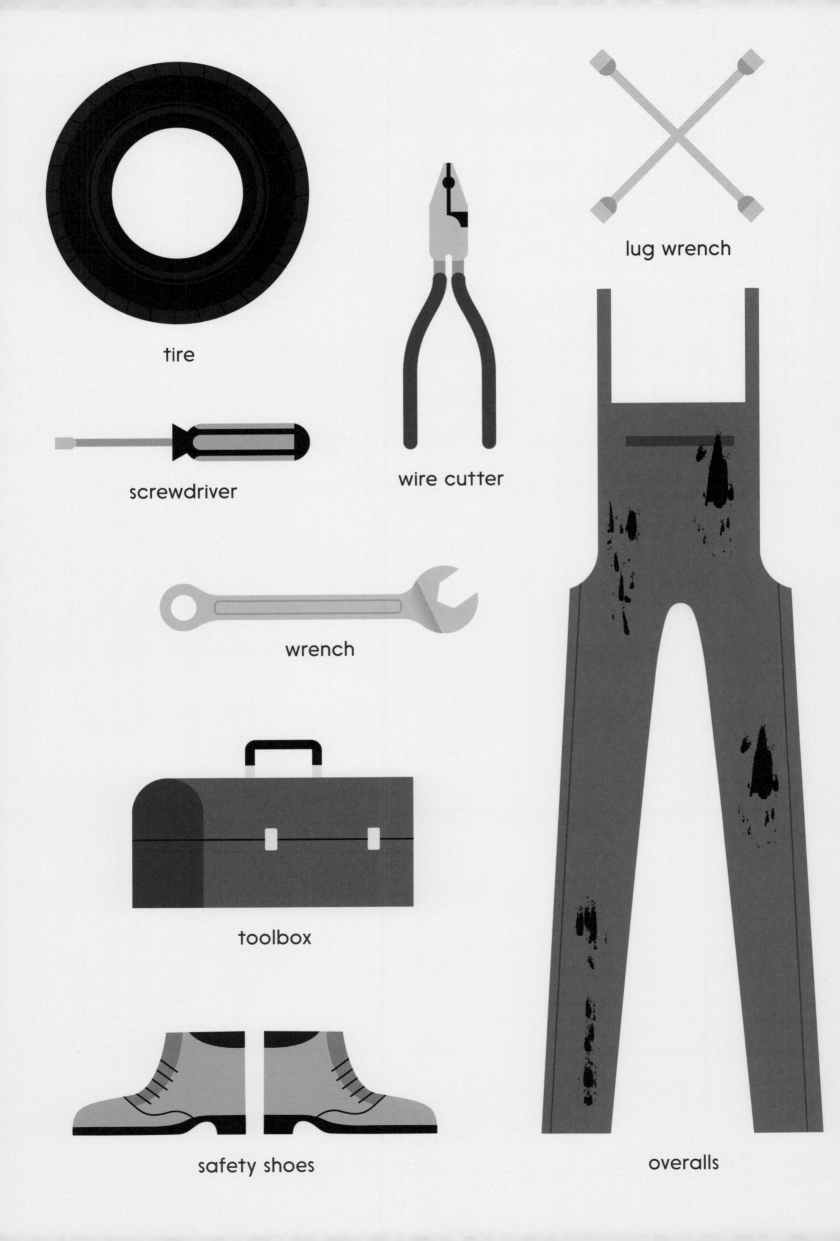

tire

screwdriver

wire cutter

wrench

toolbox

safety shoes

lug wrench

overalls

MECHANIC

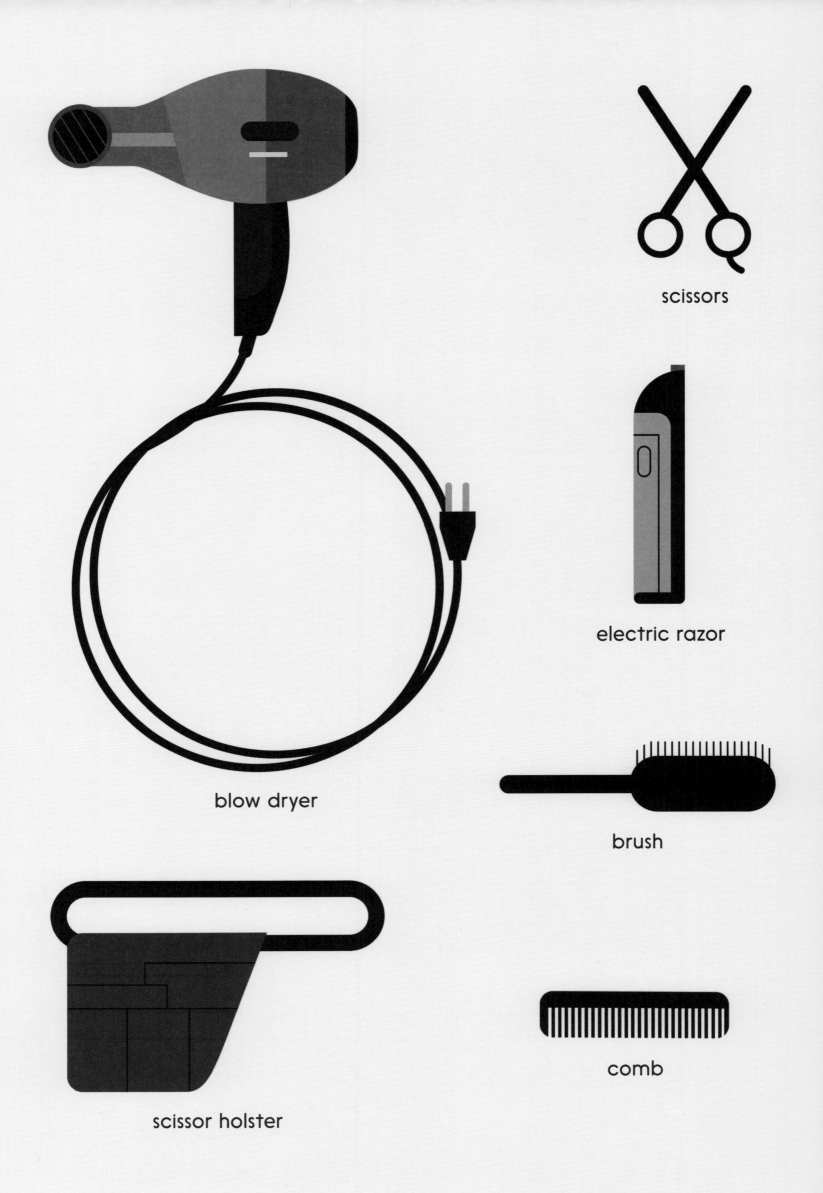

scissors

electric razor

brush

comb

blow dryer

scissor holster

HAIRDRESSER

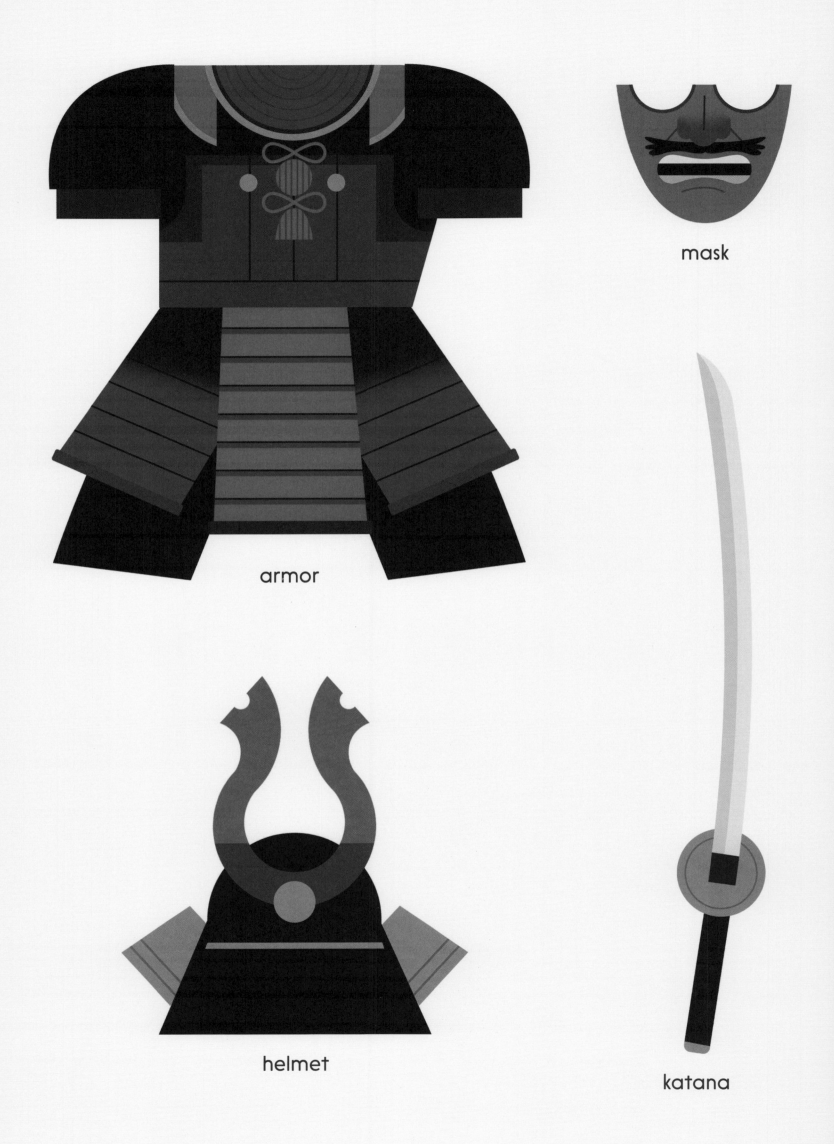

armor

mask

helmet

katana

SAMURAI

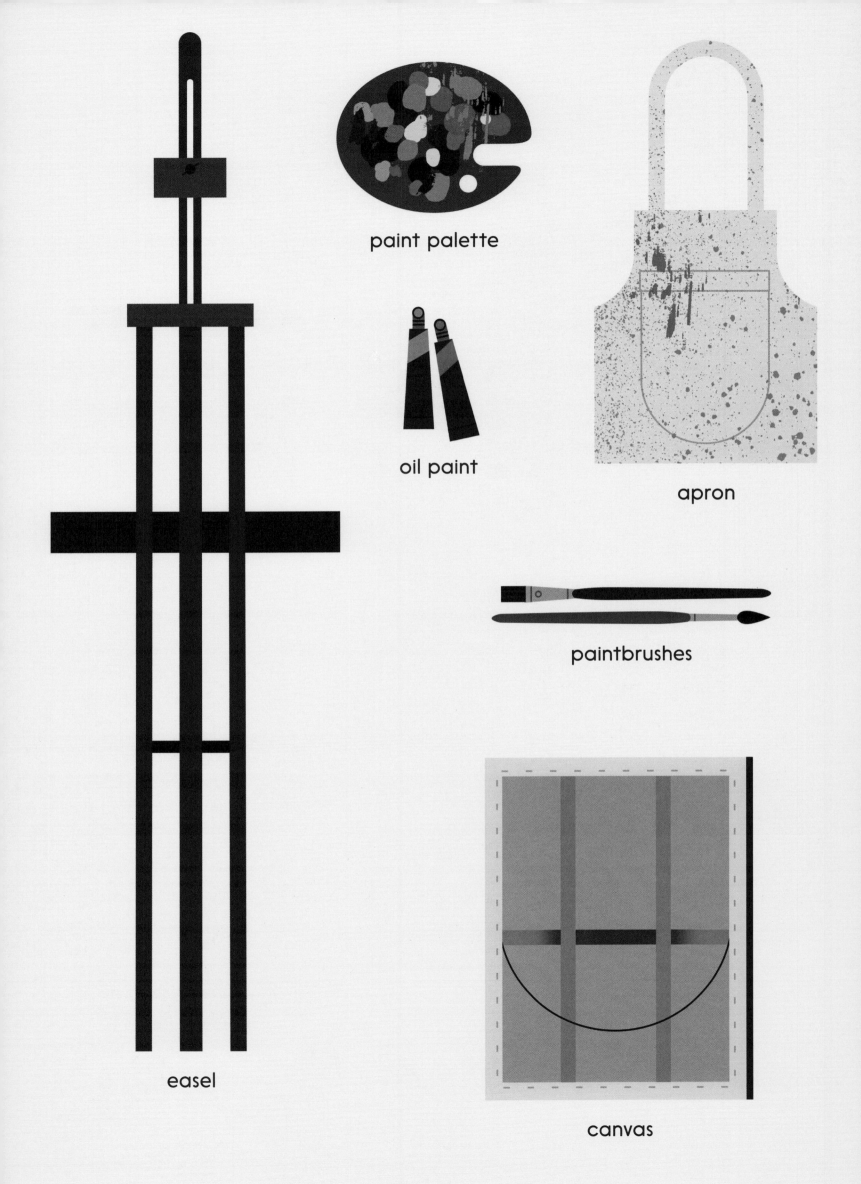

paint palette

oil paint

apron

paintbrushes

easel

canvas

PAINTER

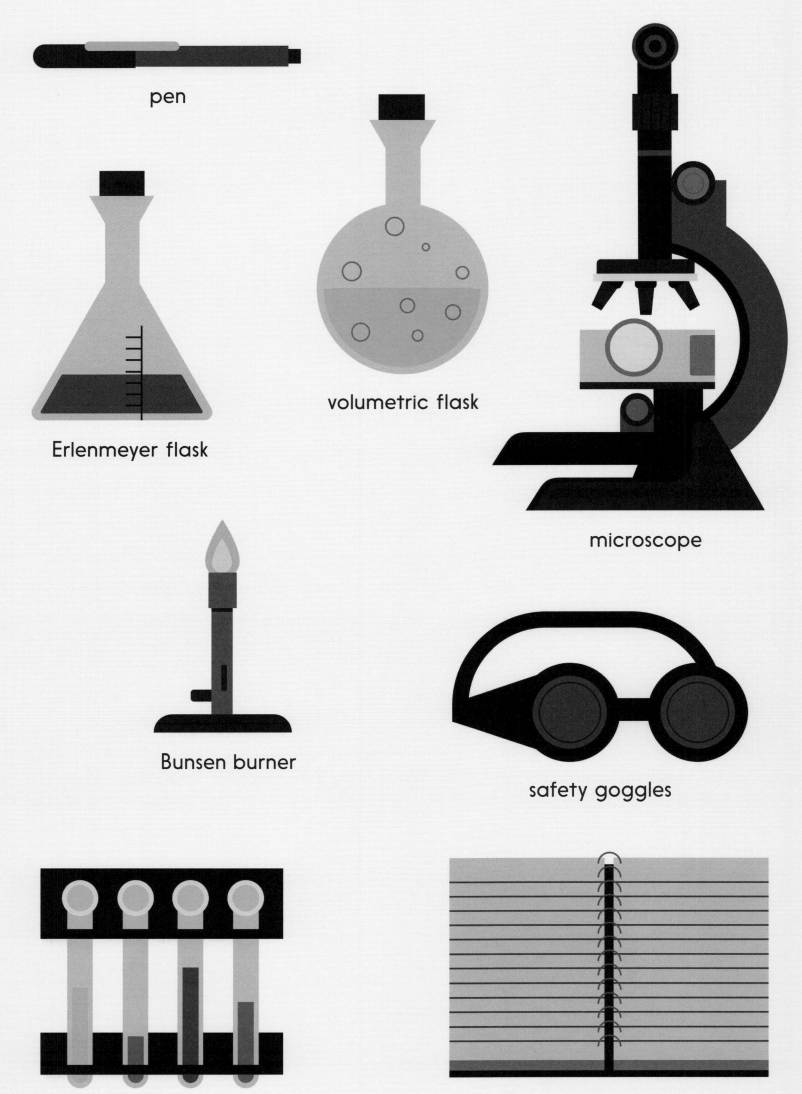

pen

Erlenmeyer flask

volumetric flask

microscope

Bunsen burner

safety goggles

test tubes

spiral notebook

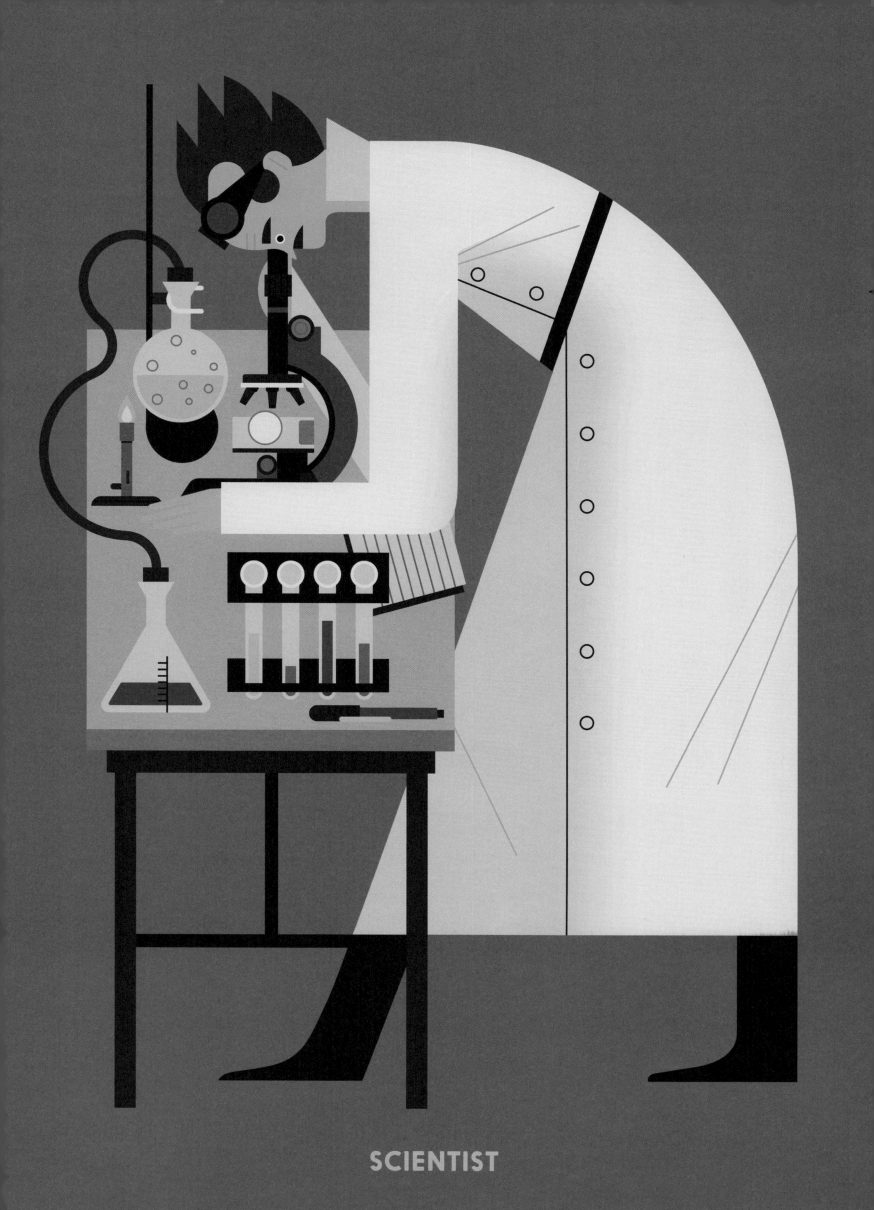

SCIENTIST

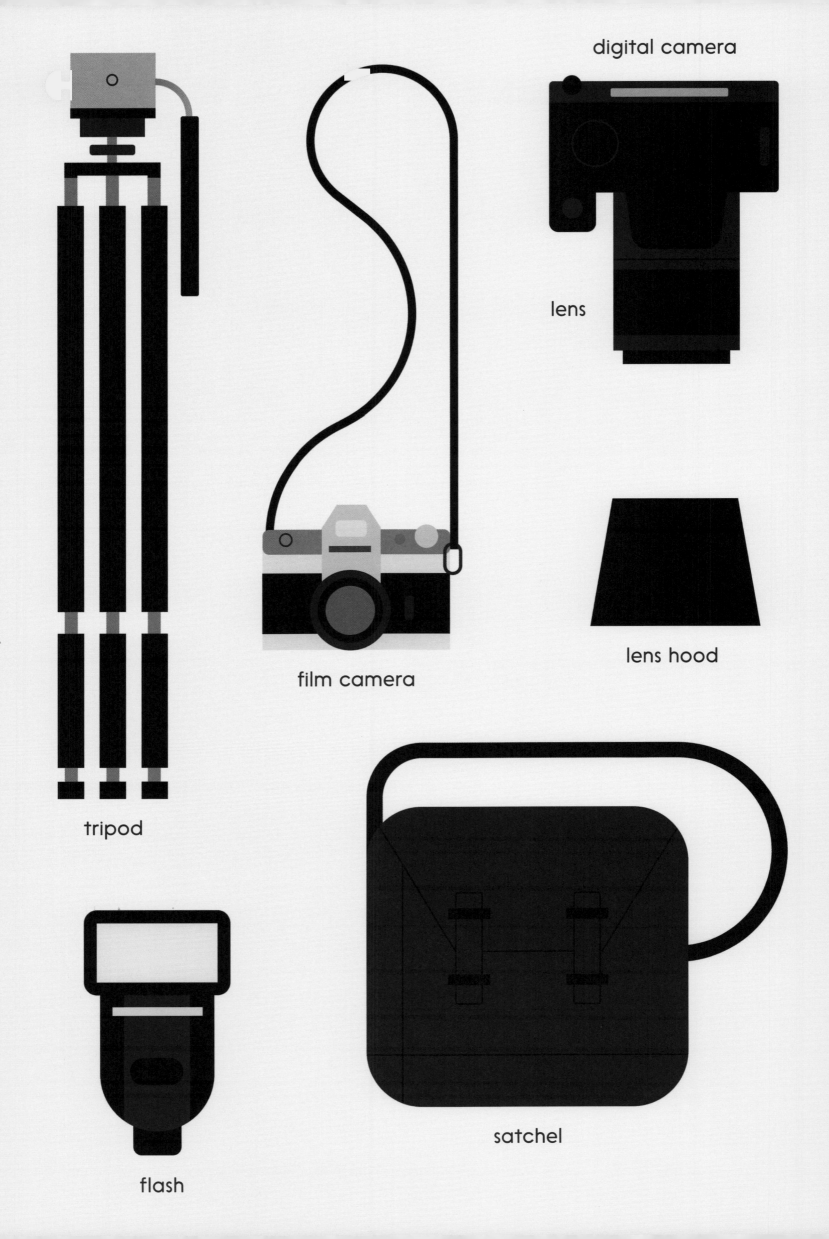

digital camera

lens

lens hood

film camera

tripod

satchel

flash

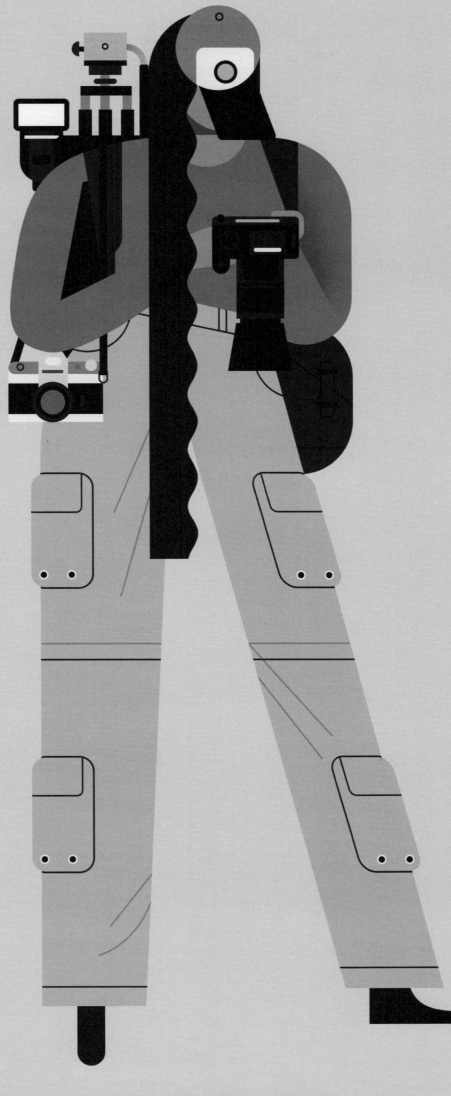

PHOTOGRAPHER

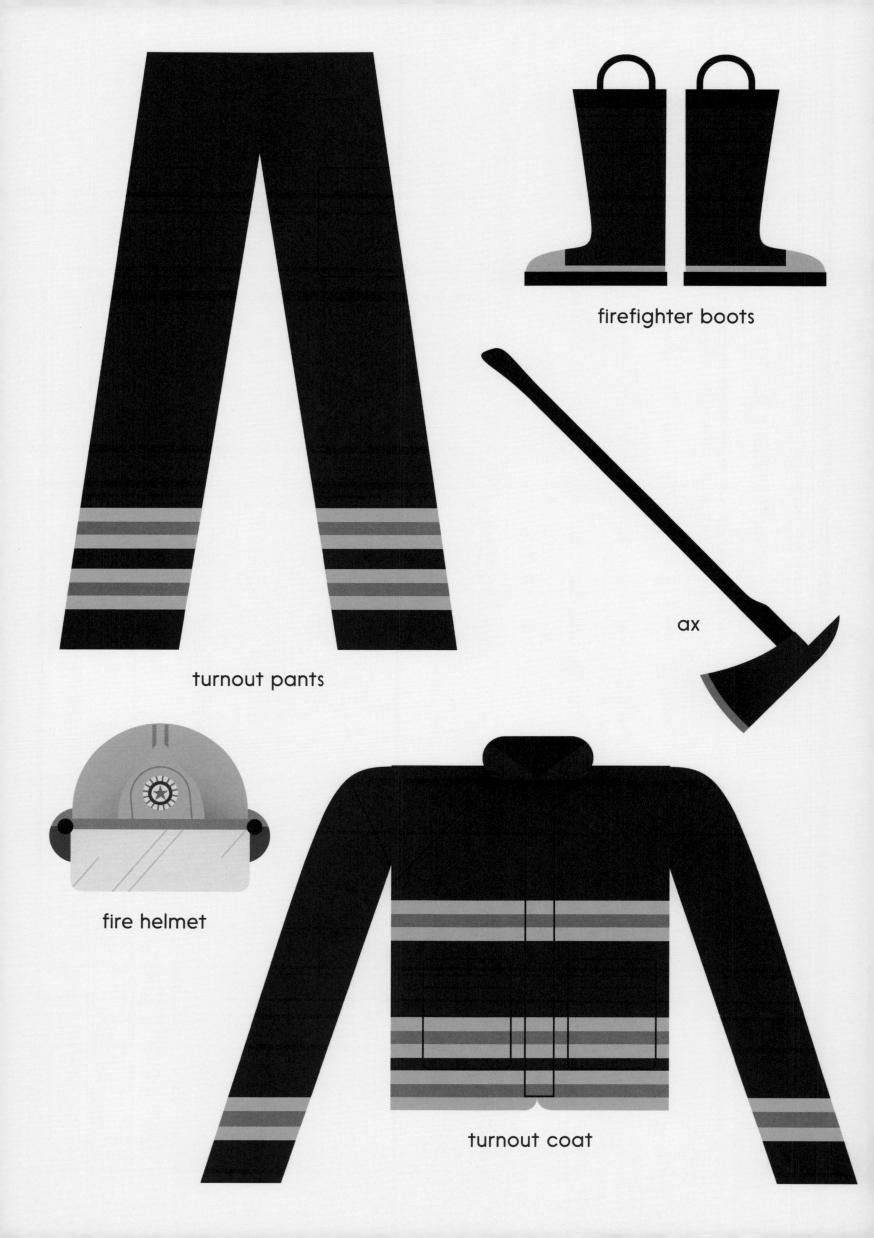

firefighter boots

turnout pants

ax

fire helmet

turnout coat

FIREFIGHTER

sleeping pad

hiking boots

sleeping bag

backpack

canteen

hat

trekking poles

HIKER

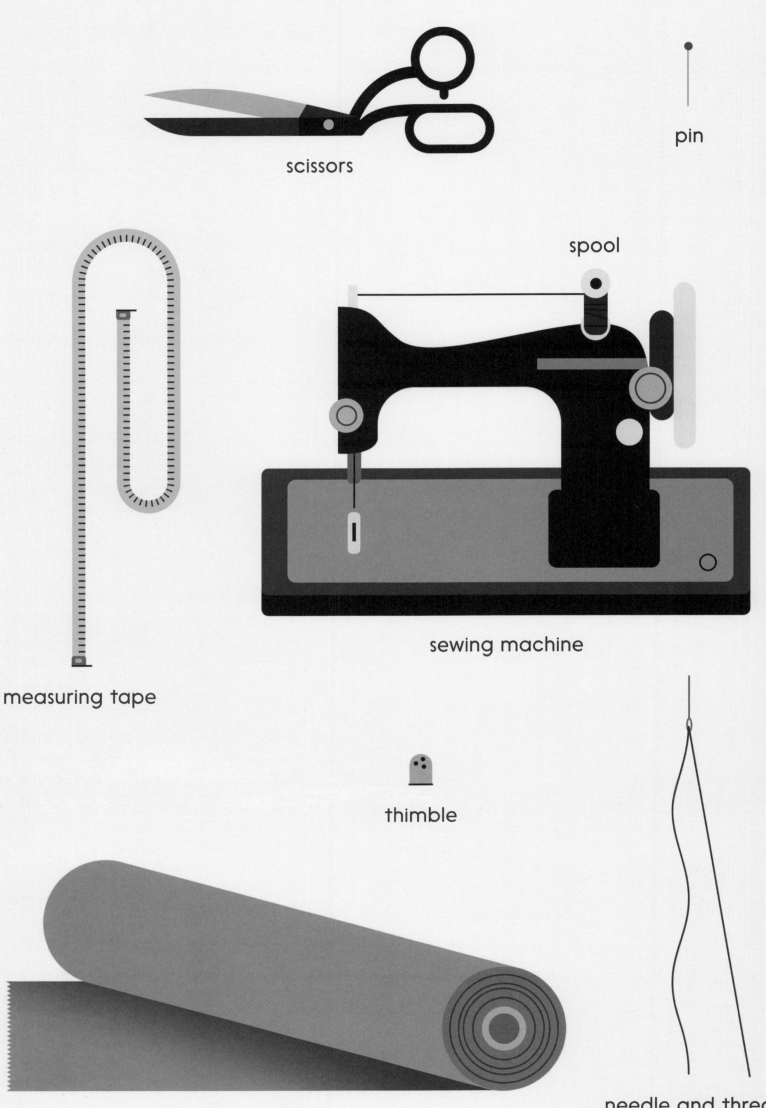

scissors

pin

spool

sewing machine

measuring tape

thimble

fabric

needle and thread

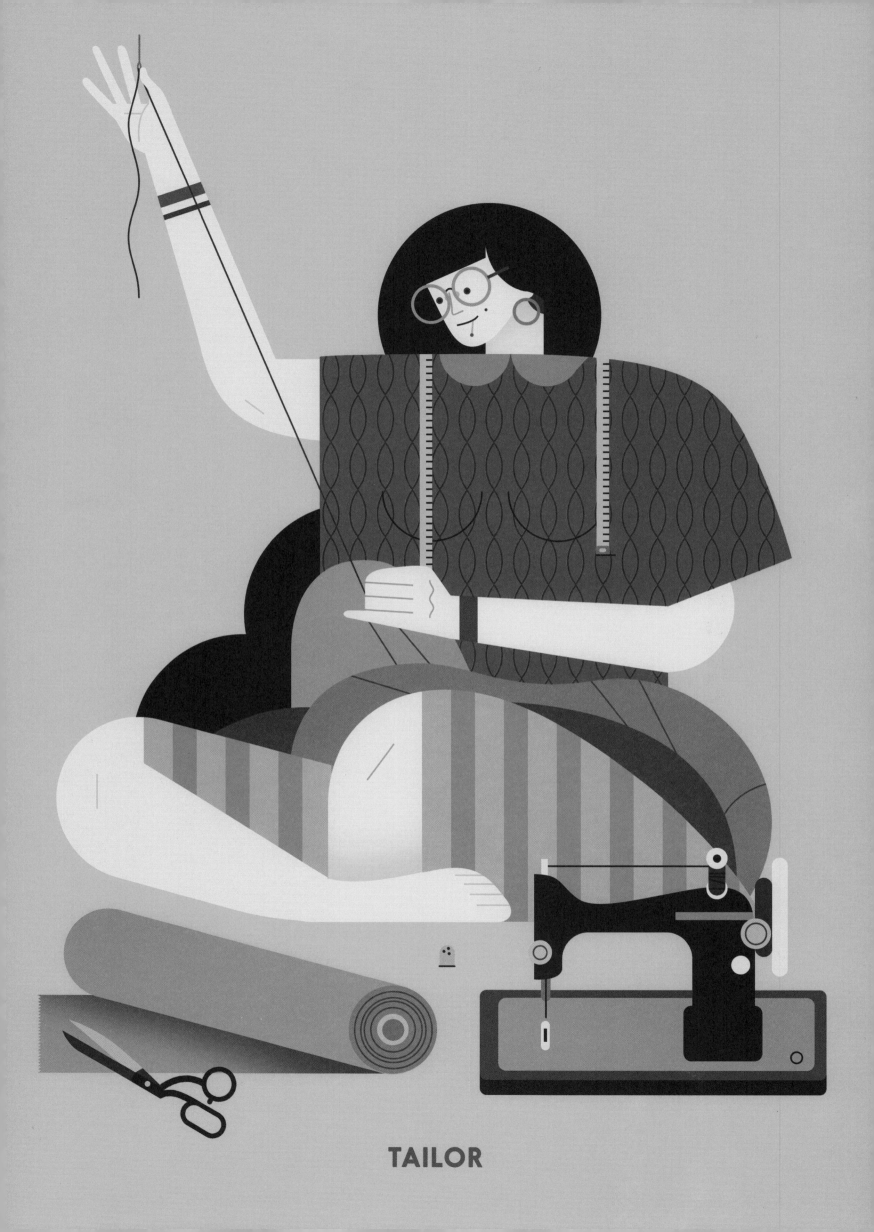

TAILOR

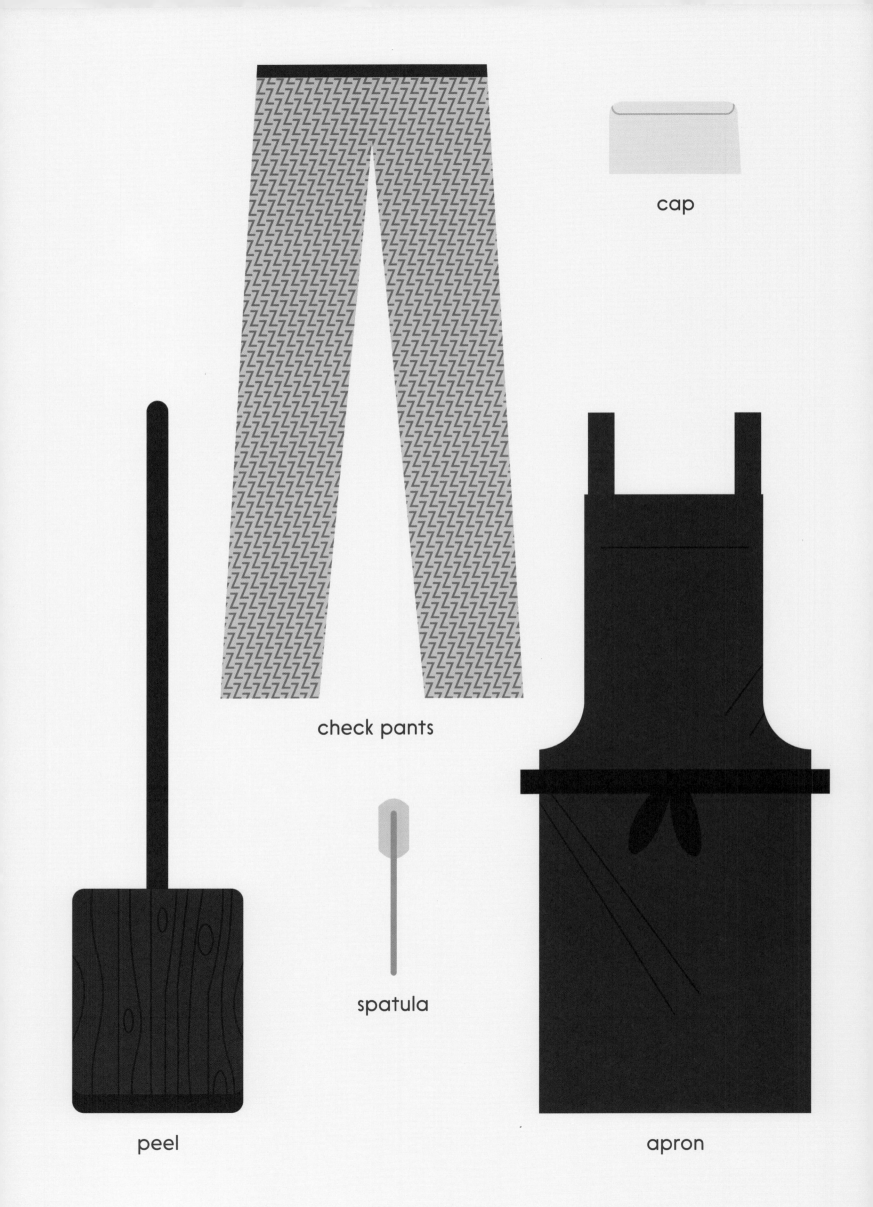

check pants

cap

peel

spatula

apron

BAKER

script

medallion

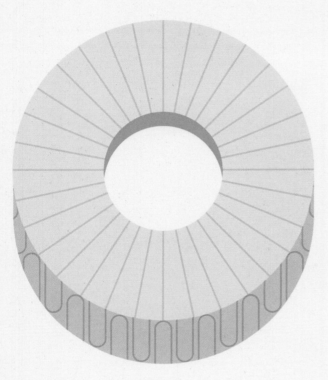

ruff

wig

false beard

prop

ACTOR

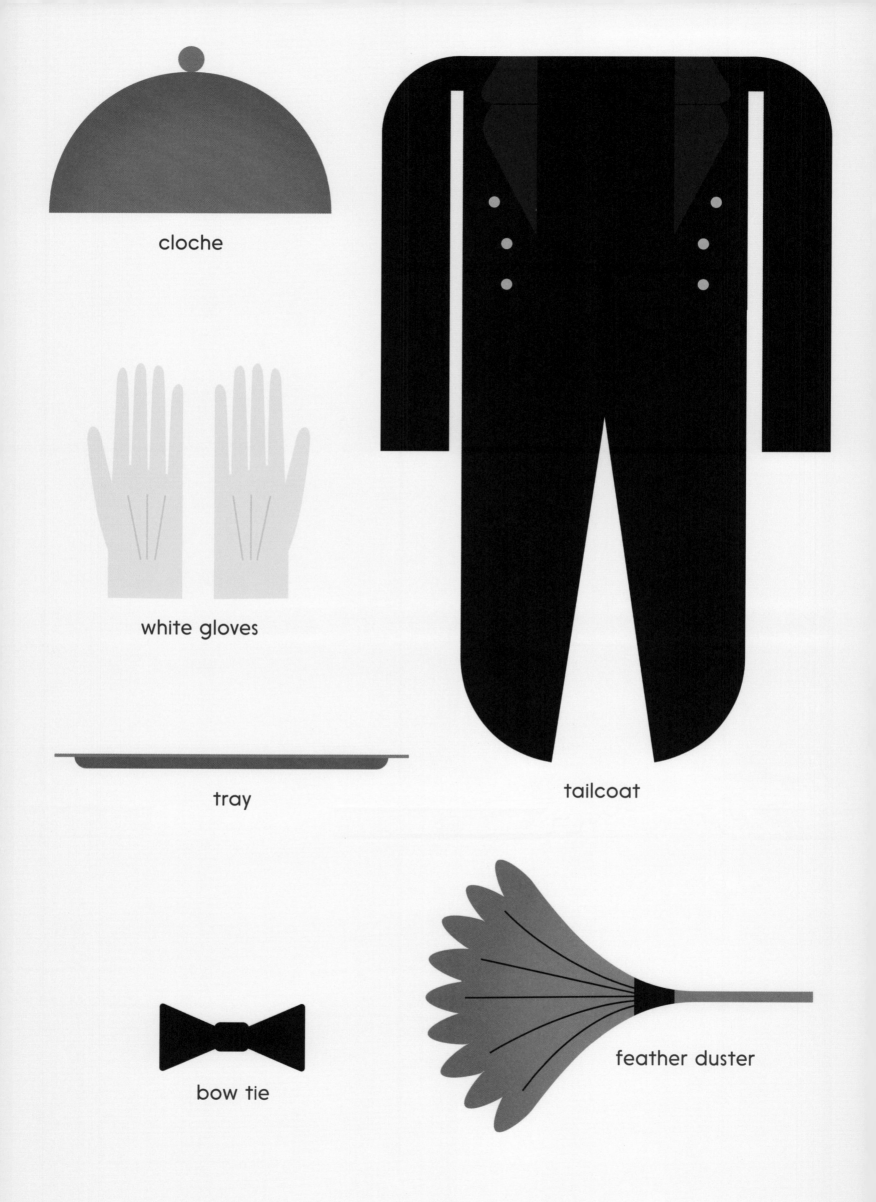

cloche

white gloves

tray

tailcoat

bow tie

feather duster

BUTLER

pistol

badge

whistle

walkie-talkie

handcuffs

police cap

baton

POLICE OFFICER

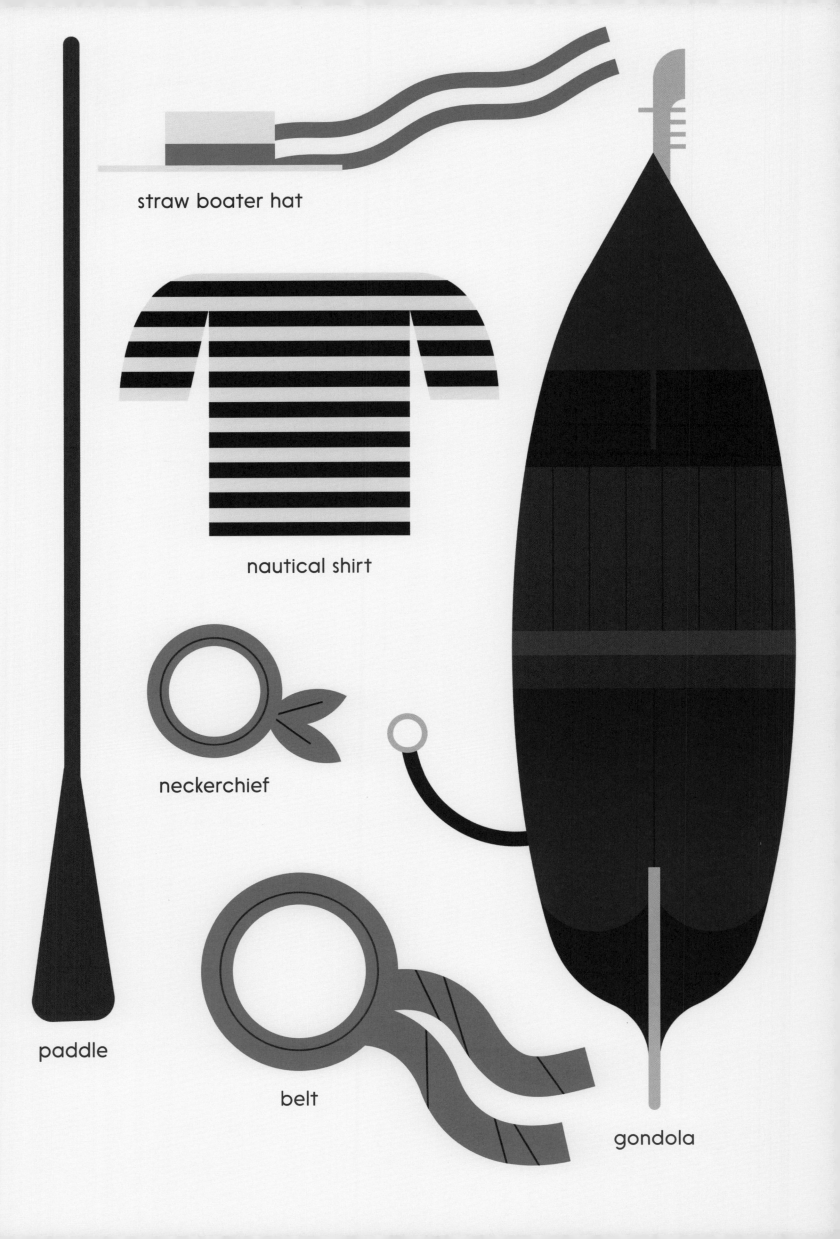

straw boater hat

nautical shirt

neckerchief

paddle

belt

gondola

GONDOLIER

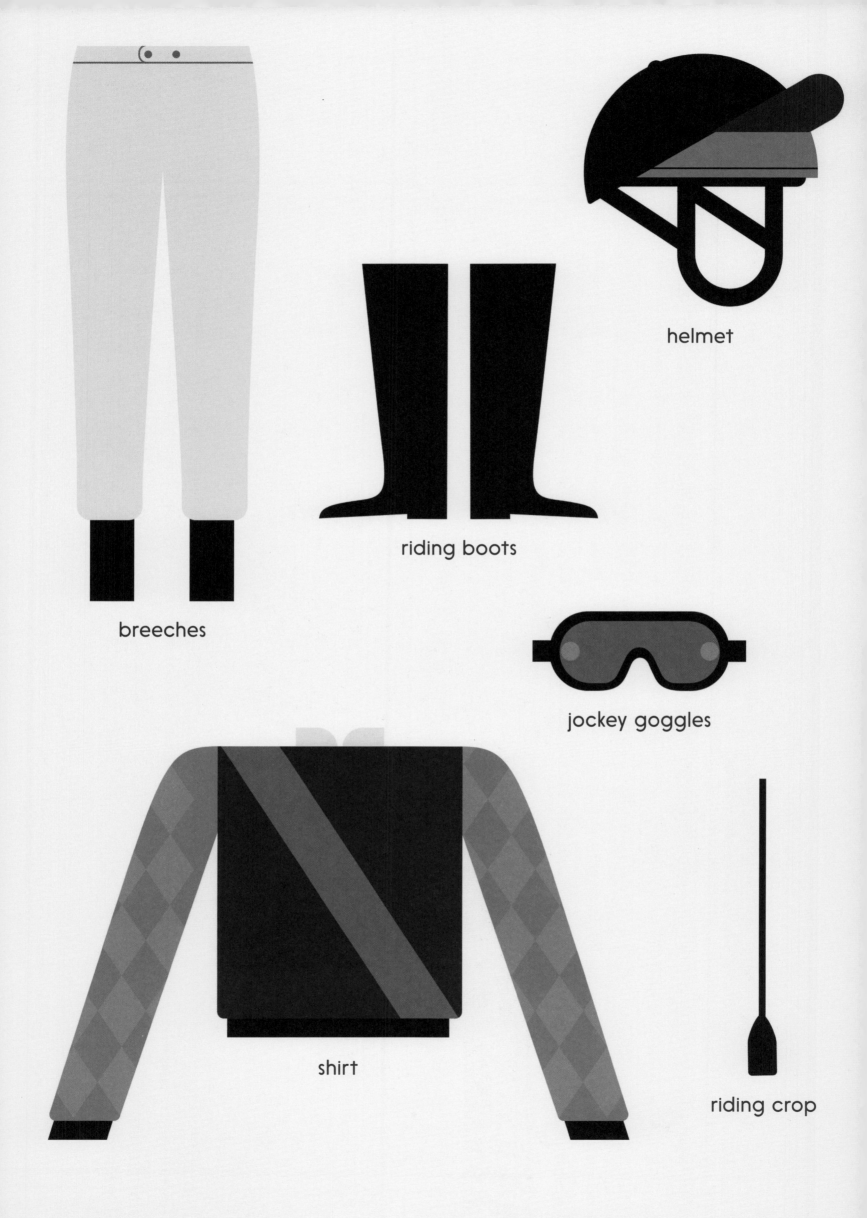

breeches

riding boots

helmet

jockey goggles

shirt

riding crop

JOCKEY

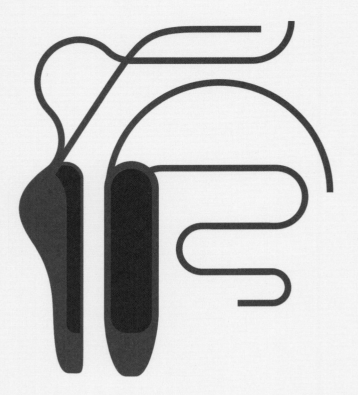

pointe shoes

leotard

tights

tutu

BALLET DANCER

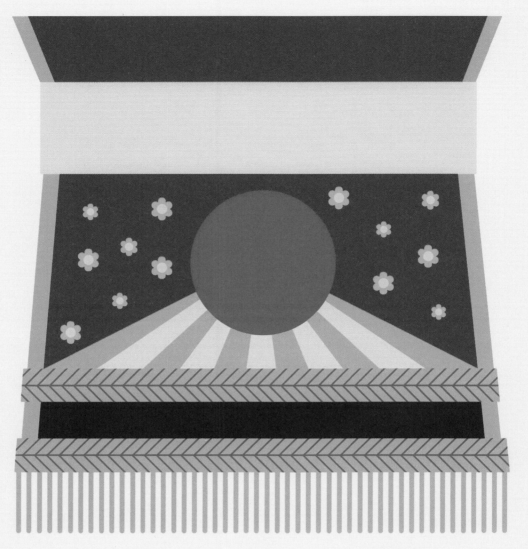

keshō-mawashi (ceremonial belt)

chonmage (topknot)

mawashi (belt)

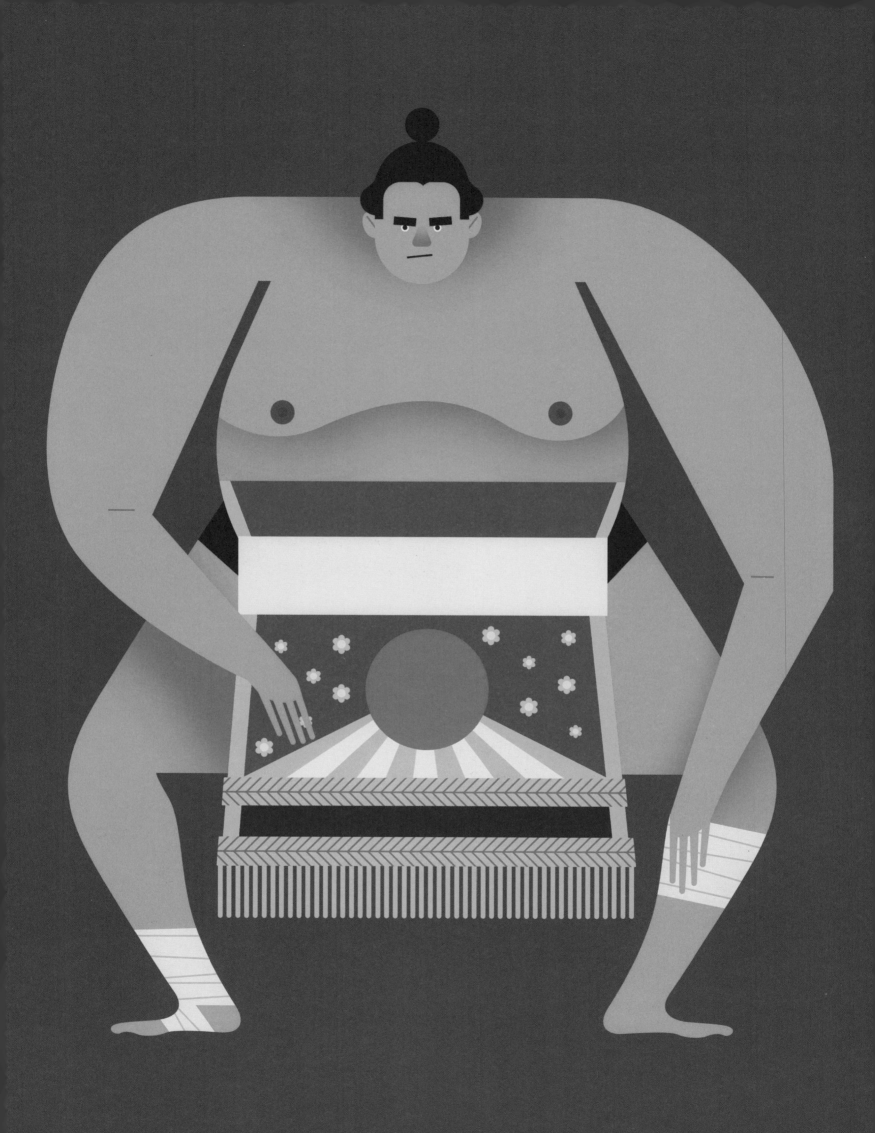

SUMO WRESTLER

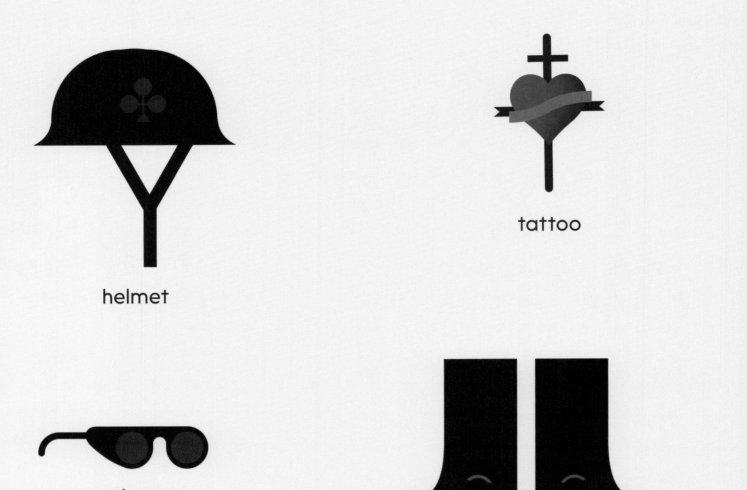

helmet

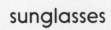

tattoo

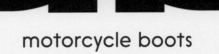

sunglasses

motorcycle boots

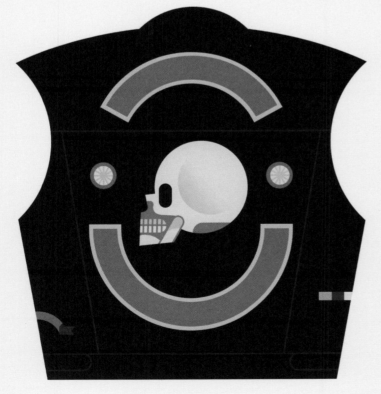

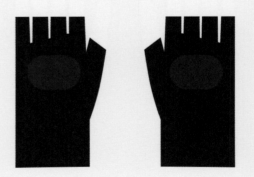

leather vest

fingerless gloves

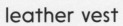

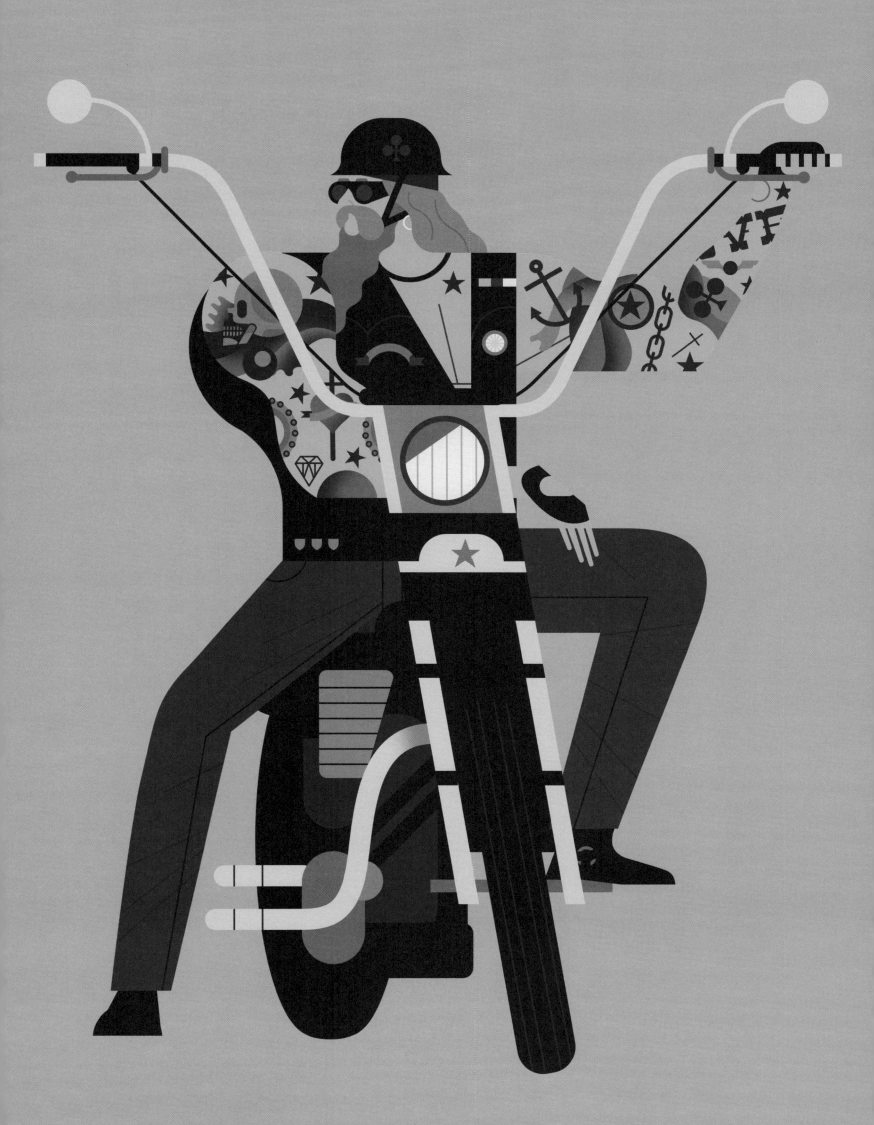

MOTORCYCLIST

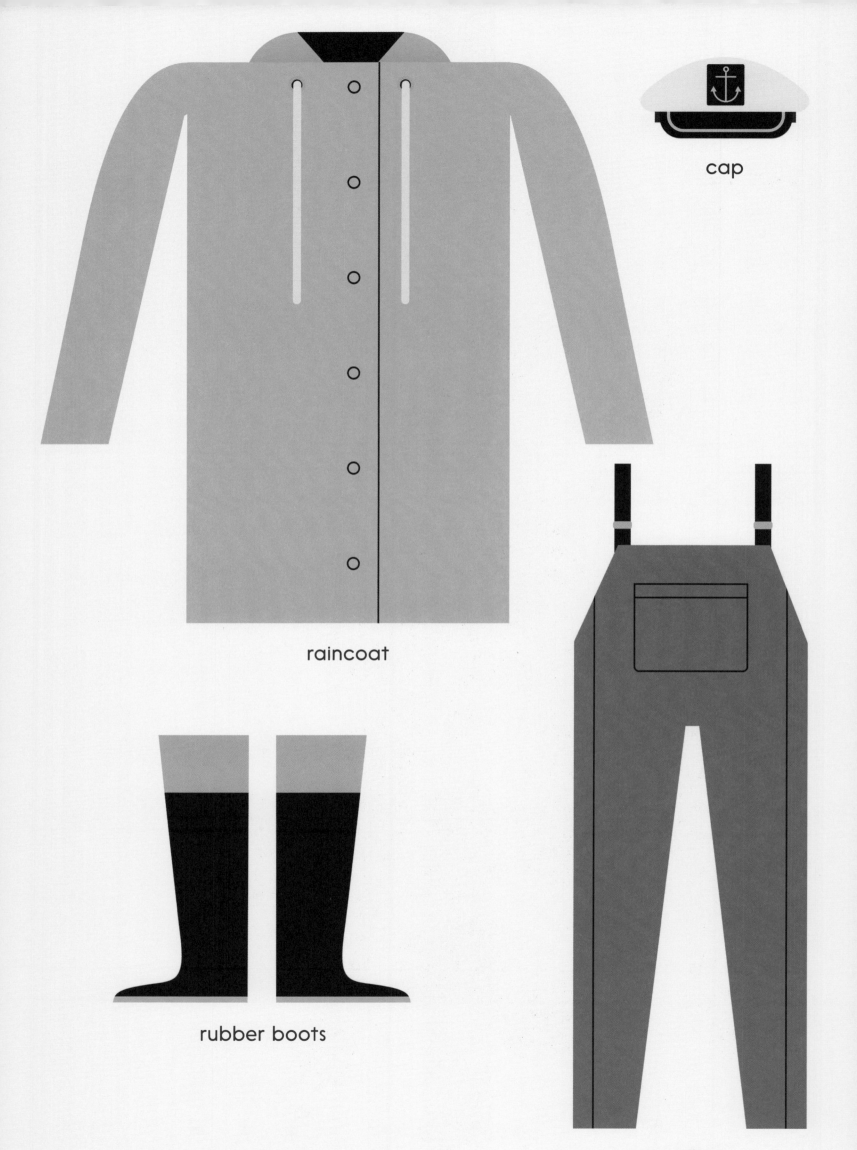

cap

raincoat

rubber boots

waders

FISHERMAN

jacket

wings

tie

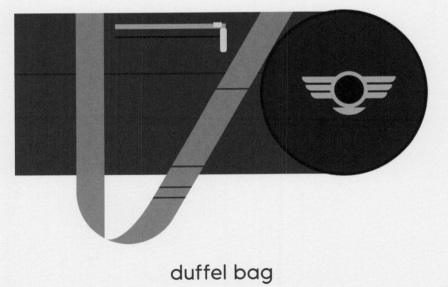

duffel bag

epaulets

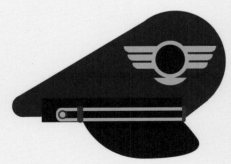

cap

PILOT

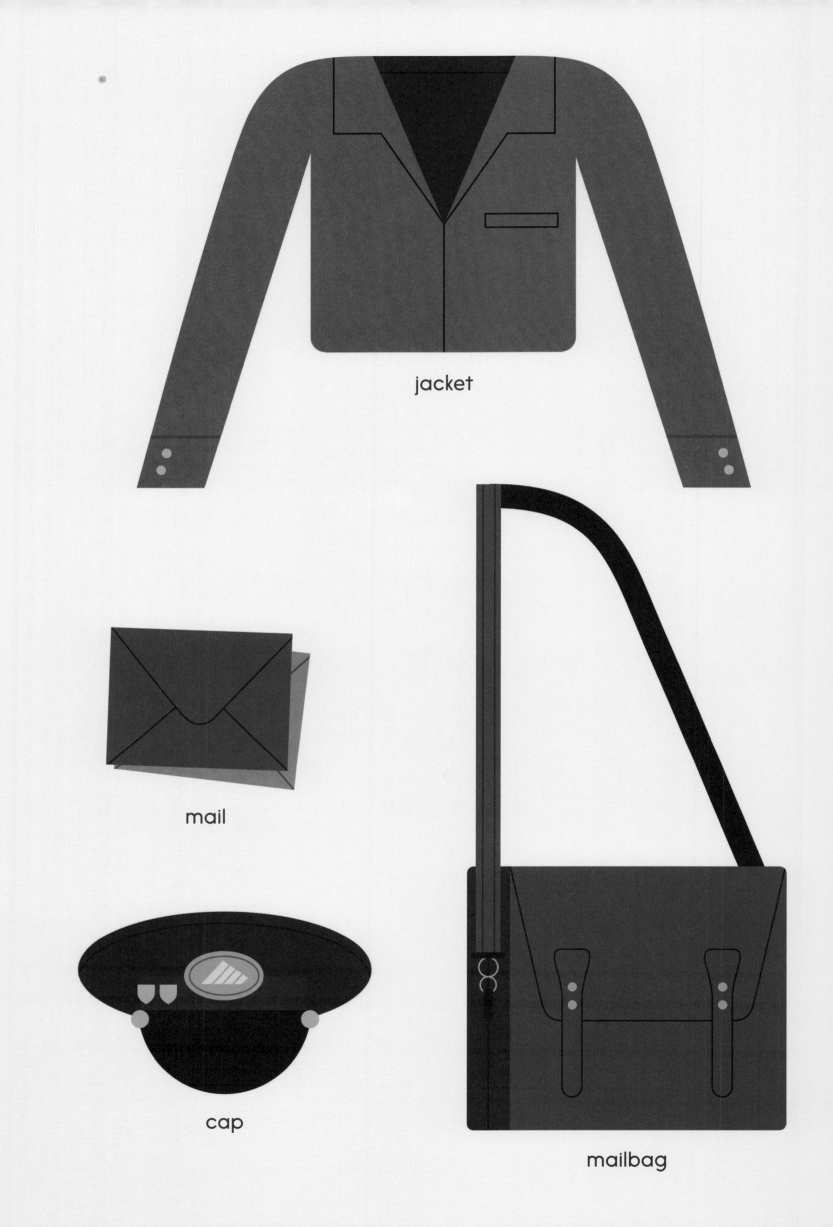

jacket

mail

cap

mailbag

MAIL CARRIER

surfboard

wetsuit

leg rope

pearl bracelet

SURFER

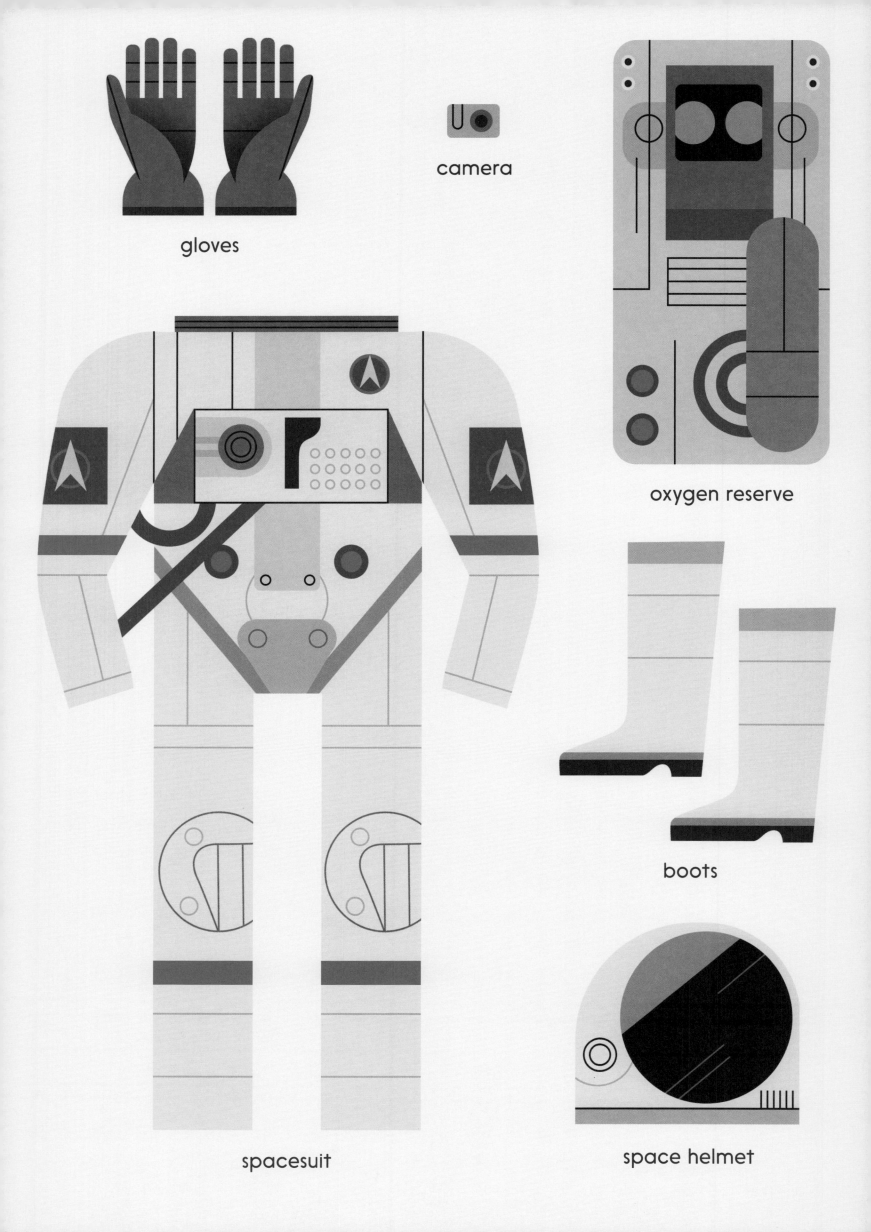

gloves

camera

oxygen reserve

boots

spacesuit

space helmet

ASTRONAUT

racing helmet

trophy

fire-retardant racing suit

boots

cap

podium

RACE CAR DRIVER

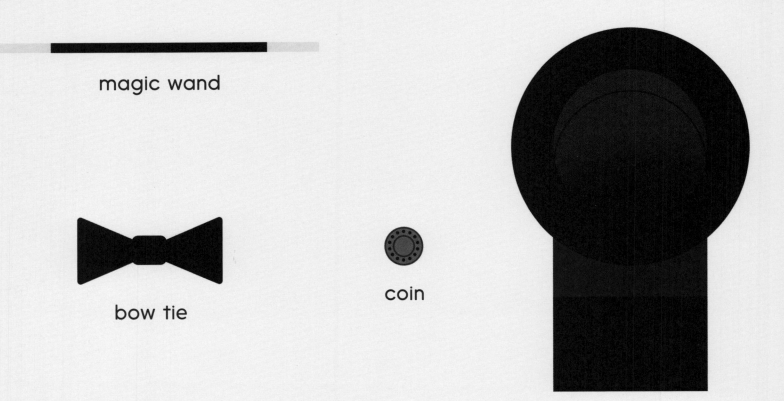

magic wand

bow tie

coin

top hat

silk square

playing cards

cape

MAGICIAN

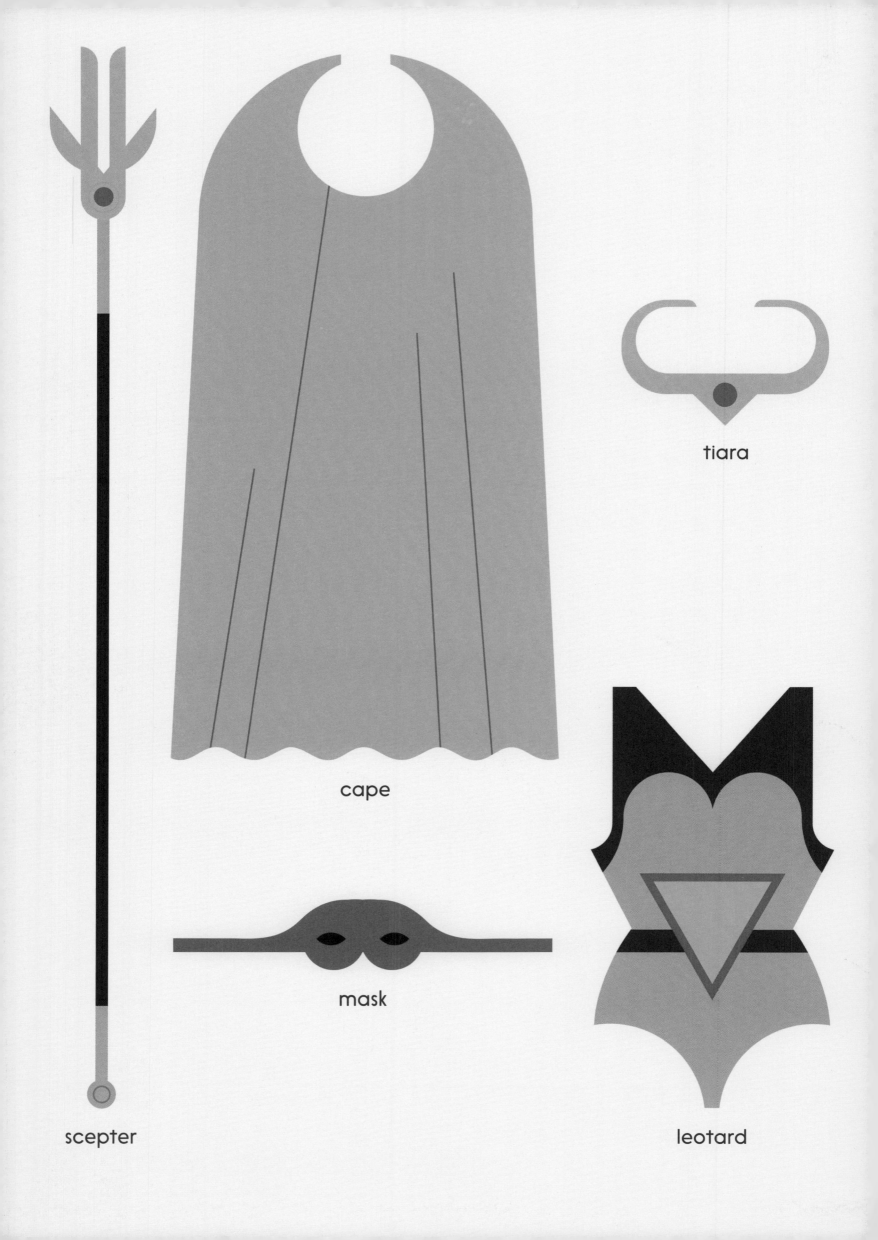

scepter

cape

tiara

mask

leotard

SUPERHERO

The Who's Who of Grown-Ups
Jobs, Hobbies and the Tools It Takes

Illustrated by Owen Davey

Translation from German to English by Elli Stuhler

Font: Nanami Rounded by Alex Haigh / Thinkdust

Printed by Toppan Leefung Printing Limited
Made in China

Published by Little Gestalten, Berlin 2020
ISBN: 978-3-89955-149-5

The French original edition "Le who's who des grandes personnes" by Éditions Milan.
© for the French original edition: Éditions Milan-France, Toulouse 2017
© for the English edition: Little Gestalten, published by Die Gestalten Verlag GmbH & Co. KG, Berlin 2020

For more information, and to order books, please visit www.little.gestalten.com

Bibliographic information published by the Deutsche Nationalbibliothek. The Deutsche Nationalbibliothek lists this
publication in the Deutsche Nationalbibliografie; detailed bibliographic data is available online at www.dnb.de